UNIVERSITY OF MINNESOTA

⤴ *Tennessee Williams*

BY GERALD WEALES

UNIVERSITY OF MINNESOTA PRESS · MINNEAPOLIS

Printed in the United States of America at
the North Central Publishing Company, St. Paul

Library of Congress Catalog Card Number: 65-64773

second printing 1970

Distributed to high schools in the United States by Webster Division
McGraw-Hill Book Company
St. Louis   New York   San Francisco   Dallas

PUBLISHED IN GREAT BRITAIN, INDIA, AND PAKISTAN BY THE OXFORD
UNIVERSITY PRESS, LONDON, BOMBAY, AND KARACHI, AND IN CANADA
BY THE COPP CLARK PUBLISHING CO. LIMITED, TORONTO

FOR RICHARD BIMONTE

who knows a play when he sees one

GERALD WEALES has written a number of books on the drama including *A Play and Its Parts* and *American Drama since World War II*, as well as a novel and two children's books. He is a member of the department of English at the University of Pennsylvania.

↗ *Tennessee Williams*

T ENNESSEE WILLIAMS once wrote: "My folks were pioneer Tennesseeans, mostly of a military and political disposition, some of them, such as Nollichucky Jack Sevier, having been famous Indian fighters when the South was being settled. I am also related to the late Senator John Sharp Williams who was a famous silver-tongued orator of Mississippi and also one of the State's best drinkers, who said when he retired that 'he would rather be a hound-dawg an' bay th' moon from his Mississippi plantation than a member of the United States Senate.'"

John Sevier did live on the Nolichucky River from 1783 to 1790 and the *Memphis Commercial Appeal* (September 27, 1932) did attribute to Senator Williams a quotation very like the one above. Tennessee Williams may well be descended from both men, but the quotation is given here not as a fact but as a symptom. It is part of a biographical statement which Williams sent to William Kozlenko, the editor of a collection of plays, *American Scenes* (1941), which included two early Williams one-acters — *This Property Is Condemned* and the now forgotten *At Liberty*. It is a young man's boast, a young writer's way of insisting that he is a silver-tongued, hard-drinking Indian fighter. It also identifies as a bona fide southerner the young dramatist whose two contributions carried the joint subtitle "Two Mississippi Plays."

Most of the biographical information that we have about Williams comes from him — from the introductory essays that were printed with his plays, from casual remarks made to interviewers — and it is probable that the facts of his life were occasionally sacrificed to an immediate effect. Many standard references still give 1914 as the year of Williams' birth although that fiction was exploded several years ago. A great many Williams characters, such as Mrs. Stone of the Roman spring, are haunted by encroaching age, but it was apparently practicality, and not vanity, that made Williams lie about the date of his birth. In 1939, in order to enter a playwriting contest that the Group Theatre was running for writers under 25, Williams knocked three years off his age, and, after he was awarded a special citation, he never bothered to put the years back. The story is told in Benjamin Nelson's *Tennessee Williams*, where there is still a little confusion about the playwright's actual and fictional ages at the time.

Williams' biography is further complicated by the fact that many commentators go to his stories and plays to find the details of his life. Some of the details are there. We know that Williams, like Tom in *The Glass Menagerie*, worked in a shoe warehouse. It is a short step from the recognition of biographical incident to the acceptance of a fictional work as a factual statement; the short story "The Resemblance between a Violin Case and a Coffin," for instance, is usually taken as an accurate re-creation of the relationship between Williams and his sister Rose. It is quite likely that a writer as self-preoccupied as Williams is (even his most casual remarks are attempts to explain or to invent his feelings) will use himself extensively in his fictional work, but there is a danger in equating fiction with fact. Amanda in *The Glass Menagerie* is almost certainly based on Williams' mother, but that certainty should not keep us from recognizing the justice of his mother's cry, in her book *Remember Me to Tom*, "I am *not* Amanda." Williams' biography, then, like T. S. Eliot's April, is a mixture involving memory and desire. It is well to keep that in mind as you read the next few paragraphs — the short version of the Tennessee Williams story.

He was born Thomas Lanier Williams on March 26, 1911, in Columbus, Mississippi. His father was a traveling salesman who spent very little time with his family and made no permanent home for them. For the first seven years of his life, Williams and his mother and sister Rose lived with Mrs. Williams' father, an Episcopalian clergyman, either in Nashville or in the various Mississippi towns — Columbus, Canton, Clarksdale — where he held parishes. In *Remember Me to Tom* there is a family portrait, in which Mrs. Williams is reading to the two children, a studio photograph of three beautiful people, a visual equivalent of the idealization which Mrs. Williams' book makes of those early years. In her story of Tom, the shocking event in his life was the move to St. Louis in 1918, when his father, now sales manager for a shoe company, brought his family to live with him; a second son, Dakin, was born in 1919. In Mrs. Williams' account of the St. Louis years, her husband appears as something of a villain — crude, stingy, drunken. It is not necessary to accept Mrs. Williams' very defensive book as completely truthful (Mr. Williams never wrote his version), but it does convey a sense of family life marked with anger, tension, separateness which might help explain the recurrent themes of Williams' plays.

If home was "not a pleasant refuge," as Williams once said, the outside world was no better. Williams recalls being teased by gangs of boys when he began to go to school. But go to school he did. He graduated from high school in January 1929, and went on to the University of Missouri that fall. He was forced to drop out after his third year and go to work for the International Shoe Company. His distaste for the job has so colored the accounts of that period that it is difficult now to know exactly what was going on in the Williams household. As the story is told, his father is once again the villain, insisting on his withdrawal from college, pushing him into the shoe company. But the year was 1932. There must have been quite a few young men who could not go to college that year and who would have considered themselves lucky to have found even a dull job which paid $65 a month. For Williams, however, his three years at the shoe company were "a living death." He escaped finally by breaking down, a collapse that is attributed variously to exhaustion, heart palpitations, and the recurrence of a childhood paralysis. After a recuperative summer with his grandparents in Memphis, he enrolled at Washington University in St. Louis, from which he was dropped in 1937. He graduated finally from the University of Iowa in 1938 and began the life of writing and wandering which has been going on — with increasing degrees of affluence — ever since.

Within the superstructure of employment and education described above, Williams was becoming a writer. He began — as what writer does not — when he was still a child; in *Remember Me to Tom*, Mrs. Williams reprints two poems which he wrote for his junior high newspaper in 1925. It is easy to call up stereotypes of the "writer" when one thinks of the young Tennessee Williams at work. Image One: the sensitive boy, uncomfortable in the public world of school and the private world of home, taking refuge in his typewriter. Image Two (borrowed from *The Glass Menagerie*): the compulsive poet, trapped by the prosaic world, scribbling lyric effusions on shoebox tops. There is probably truth in both these images. "I write from my own tensions," Williams once told a reporter from *Newsweek*. "For me, this is a form of therapy." From most of Williams' statements about his work, it is evident that for him writing is both home and healing, a way of making order out of disorder. There is, however, another, an important side to Williams the writer.

In a 1960 interview with Arthur Gelb in the *New York Times*, he speaks of his "desire for success": "I want to reach a mass audience." From the beginning, Williams has been not only the

8

"poet," sending messages out of his own isolation, but the professional writer in search of an audience and commercial success. Amusingly enough, this side of him appears in embryonic form in the teen-age Williams. In 1927, pretending to be an unhappily married traveling salesman (a bouquet for Daddy?), the sixteen-year-old boy won third prize in a *Smart Set* contest, "Can a Good Wife Be a Good Sport?"; his entry, which answers *no* to the question, is reprinted in *Remember Me to Tom*. In 1928, his first professionally published story appeared in the August issue of *Weird Tales*. In 1929, when the university newspaper interviewed him, as a freshman whose name had already appeared in national magazines, Williams said that Louis Bromfield was his favorite author. With a best-selling novelist to look up to and with popular magazines — slicks and pulps — as his goal, Williams was obviously already thinking of himself as a professional; his announced ambition was to go to the School of Journalism.

It was later, during the Washington University years, that Williams began to read intensively in those writers whose marks can be found on much of his work — D. H. Lawrence, Hart Crane, Lorca, Rimbaud, Rilke, Melville. It was then presumably, in his association with a group of students with literary ambitions, that his "desire for success" was transformed. Without losing the original impulse toward fame and fortune, Williams the writer acquired his double, Williams the artist. There is room in Williams the man for both figures. There is no reason why both the *Newsweek* and the *Times* quotations cannot be taken as true. The kind of revisions that he has done on his plays over the years displays both sides of him; he rewrites in an attempt to find the play implicit in the original material (as when he made *Orpheus Descending* out of *Battle of Angels*), but he also rewrites in an attempt to get the audience he would like to have, as when, following Elia Kazan's suggestions, he provided a new third act for *Cat on a Hot Tin Roof*, one which changed the meaning of the play).

Tennessee Williams' career as a playwright got under way in earnest in 1935, during the summer he spent in Memphis. He had written plays earlier when he was at the University of Missouri, but the production of *Cairo! Shanghai! Bombay!* by a small summer theater seems to have given him the immediate impetus to turn out more plays. This comedy (of which a Memphis friend, Dorothy Shapiro, was co-author), like most of his youthful plays, has never been printed. His second play to be produced was something called *The Magic Tower* which was done in 1936 by a theater group in Webster Groves, a St. Louis suburb. That year he became associated with The Mummers, a lively St. Louis theater group under the direction of Willard Holland, whom Williams warmly praises in his introduction to *27 Wagons Full of Cotton*, "Something Wild . . ." For them, he wrote a one-acter, *Headlines*, to serve as a curtain-raiser for an Armistice Day production of Irwin Shaw's *Bury the Dead*. Within the next two years, The Mummers produced two full-length Williams plays, *Candles in the Sun* and *Fugitive Kind* (which should not, for all its title, be confused with the movie version of *Orpheus Descending*); a third play, *Not about Nightingales*, was about to be done in 1938 when the group died of economic malnutrition. From the description of these and other plays of the period, it is clear that social criticism, which runs under the surface of most of Williams' work, was presented overtly, even blatantly. *Headlines* was obviously a pacifist tract, and *Me, Vashya!* written at the same time, was about the decade's favorite monster, the munitions maker. *Candles in the Sun*, which concerned coal miners in Alabama, was described by a reviewer on the *St. Louis Post-Dispatch* as a play about "poverty, degeneracy, accidents on the fifth level below ground, a strike and a brutal murder, ending with beans for every-body, hope and the singing of 'solidarity forever.'"

In 1939, Tennessee Williams (who had by this time dropped the Thomas Lanier) ceased to be simply a local playwright. That year, he bundled together most of his collected works, including a group of one-acters called *American Blues*, and shipped them off to the Group Theatre contest. The judges — Harold Clurman, Irwin Shaw, and Molly Day Thacher — gave him a special award, as the citation says, for "a group of three sketches which constitute a full-length play." At this point, no one seems quite certain what plays made up *American Blues*, although Mrs. Williams, in her book, mentions *Moony's Kid Don't Cry, The Dark Room,* and *The Case of the Crushed Petunias.* All three of them appear in the Dramatists Play Service collection called *American Blues*, published in 1948, but *Petunias* carries the dateline: Key West, February 1941. In any case, they have neither stylistic nor themat-ic similarities and could hardly be considered as related sketches.

The most important result of the Group Theatre prize was that Williams got himself an agent, Audrey Wood, who had faith in him and worked hard for him. One of her first official acts was to get him a Rockefeller Fellowship, which gave him money enough to work comfortably, to rewrite *Battle of Angels*, which was to be his first play to receive a major theatrical production. At this time, 1940, he attended a seminar on playwriting which John Gassner and Theresa Helburn conducted at the New School in associa-tion with the Theatre Guild's Bureau of New Plays. Apparently largely as a result of Gassner's urging, the Theatre Guild produced *Battle of Angels*. It opened in Boston on December 30, 1940, with Miriam Hopkins in the lead and, after mechanical and spiritual crises, the play closed without ever getting to New York. Its open-ing night was a fiasco, in part because a smoke-making machine got out of control, but its chief difficulty in Boston was that it hit censorship trouble during the second week, presumably because someone decided that it was blasphemous. Although the Theatre Guild turned down a second revision of the play in 1941, Williams' career as a playwright — at least as a writer of short plays — was an active one in the early 1940's. *The Long Goodbye* was performed by students at the New School in 1940 and short, Williams plays were published not only in the Kozlenko volume mentioned at the beginning of this essay, but in many of the Margaret Mayorga collections of *The Best Short Plays* — in 1940, 1941, 1942, 1944, 1945.

The Glass Menagerie opened in Chicago on December 26, 1944, and in New York on March 31, 1945. The play ran for more than a year. Tennessee Williams had arrived. From that time on, his career is a matter of public record. He has averaged rather more than a play every two years: *You Touched Me!* (1945); *A Streetcar Named Desire* (1947); *Summer and Smoke* (1948); *The Rose Tattoo* (1951); *Camino Real* (1953); *Cat on a Hot Tin Roof* (1955); *Orpheus Descending* (1957); *Suddenly Last Summer* (1958); *Sweet Bird of Youth* (1959); *Period of Adjustment* (1960); *The Night of the Iguana* (1961); *The Milk Train Doesn't Stop Here Anymore* (1963; revised 1964). The dates in each case are those of the Broadway (or off-Broadway, for *Suddenly Last Summer*) productions. In June of 1964, *The Eccentricities of a Nightingale* was played in a summer theater in Nyack, New York, and, as this is being written, a Williams double bill, *Slapstick Tragedy* (*The Mutilated* and *The Gnädiges Fräulein*), has been tentatively scheduled for production on Broadway for fall 1965. In a note to the published *Nightingale*, a completely new play based on *Summer and Smoke*, Williams says that the new version was written shortly before the English production of the earlier play, which would seem to indicate that the *Nightingale* has been sitting quietly in its cage since 1951. Because of his habit of revision and his sensible

12

desire to see his plays performed on stage before they face a New York audience, it is always difficult to place an exact time of composition. *You Touched Me!,* which Williams wrote with Donald Windham, was performed in 1944 in both Cleveland and Pasadena and certainly, in its first form, predates *The Glass Menagerie. Summer and Smoke* was performed at Margo Jones' theater in Dallas in 1947; a version of *Sweet Bird* was put on in Florida as early as 1956; many of the recent plays have been tried out at the festival in Spoleto, Italy. *Orpheus,* of course, is *Battle of Angels* done over, and *Camino Real* is an extended treatment of *Ten Blocks on the Camino Real,* first published in 1948.

If we take 100 performances as a respectable run for a play in New York, Williams has had only three failures: *Camino Real, Orpheus Descending,* and *Milk Train* (in both versions). Of these, *Camino* and *Orpheus* have been revived off-Broadway, and *Summer and Smoke,* which just made 100 performances in its original production, was an outstanding off-Broadway success at the Circle in the Square in 1952. His greatest commercial and critical successes have been *The Glass Menagerie, A Streetcar Named Desire, Cat on a Hot Tin Roof,* and *The Night of the Iguana.* These plays not only had the longest runs, but they all received the Drama Critics Circle Award and two of them (*Streetcar* and *Cat*) were given the Pulitzer Prize. While the reception of his plays was presumably satisfying the playwright's "desire for success" (and incidentally making him a rich man), the artist in him could take comfort in the knowledge that he had gained a reputation as one of the handful of American playwrights who could be considered serious dramatists. The two most apparent manifestations of that recognition can be found in Europe, where he is widely produced, and in American colleges, where his plays (particularly *The Glass Menagerie*) have become part of the standard curriculum. Although his critical reputation is based on his long plays, he has published two collections of short plays, 27 *Wagons Full of Cotton and Other One-Act Plays* (1946, 1953) and *American Blues* (1948), and a scattering of uncollected works of which the best known, *I Rise in Flame, Cried the Phoenix* (1951), has D. H. Lawrence as its hero.

There is probably no American playwright since 1920 — with the exception of Eugene O'Neill — who has not written for the movies as well as for the stage. Tennessee Williams spent six months in 1943 as a contract writer for MGM, turning out scripts that were never filmed; it was during this period that he wrote *The Gentleman Caller*, an original screenplay which he later turned into *The Glass Menagerie*. Since the success of that play, he has had a hand in six films, five of them adaptations of his plays. He was co-author of the screenplays for *The Glass Menagerie* (1950, with Peter Berneis), *The Rose Tattoo* (1955, with Hal Kanter), *Suddenly Last Summer* (1959, with Gore Vidal), and *The Fugitive Kind* (1960, with Meade Roberts). His two most important films are those on which he was sole author — *A Streetcar Named Desire* (1951) and *Baby Doll* (1956). Both of these films, which Elia Kazan directed, are works of distinction. *Streetcar* is the most successful transfer of a Williams play from stage to screen, and *Baby Doll* contains, in Archie Lee Meighan, one of the funniest and most horrifying of Williams' comic grotesques. Williams told the *New York Times* in 1960 that *The Fugitive Kind* was the last film he would ever write. He has so far held to that resolution.

"I am not a good writer. Sometimes I am a very bad writer indeed." So Williams wrote in an essay published with *Battle of Angels* in *Pharos*. He was attempting to explain his attraction to the theater where, presumably, the objectivity of the genre would keep him from the romantic and subjective excess that he falls prey to in his stories and poems. His lines may be taken as an

14

accurate summation of his talent for fiction and poetry. Yet, he has published two volumes of short stories, *One Arm* (1948) and *Hard Candy* (1954); a short novel, *The Roman Spring of Mrs. Stone* (1950); and a collection of poems, *In the Winter of Cities* (1956, 1964). The novel is a somewhat tiresome account of an aging ex-actress who passes from being a seller to becoming a buyer of youth and beauty; it is interesting primarily because its heroine resembles so many of Williams' stage heroines, particularly Alexandra in *Sweet Bird of Youth*. Both the stories and the poems are shot through with a kind of fuzzy mysticism which must share the page with a very specific depiction of perversion (Oliver in "One Arm" dies in the electric chair with the letters from his male lovers between his legs). Most of the stories and poems are uninteresting except as they relate to the plays. Lines from the poems find their way into the dialogue of the plays; for instance, one poem, "The Beanstalk Country," contributes a useful metaphor to *Sweet Bird of Youth*. Many of the stories are early workouts for later plays: "Portrait of a Girl in Glass" for *The Glass Menagerie*, which it greatly resembles; "Three Players of a Summer Game" for *Cat on a Hot Tin Roof*; "Man Bring This Up Road" for *The Milk Train Doesn't Stop Here Anymore*; "The Night of the Iguana," which gave its name, its heroine, its setting, and its lizard to the play. Williams, then, is a literary jack-of-all-trades, sending messages of all kinds back from the beanstalk country where he has seen the ogre, but as a poet or a writer of fiction he is working with a jammed communications system. In the rest of this pamphlet, which will attempt to describe what Williams is trying to say and how he goes about it, the plays will necessarily be center stage.

"I have never been able to say what was the theme of my play and I don't think I have ever been conscious of writing with a theme in mind." So Tennessee Williams wrote in "Questions without Answers," an article in the *New York Times* in 1948, which, as usual, was part aesthetics, part advertisement for the play about to open — *Summer and Smoke* in this case. "Usually when asked about a theme, I look vague and say, 'It's a play about life.'" The lines, of course, are defensive. No writer likes to think that a work of his can safely be paraphrased and, if it is to be summed up in a sentence or two, he does not want to do the job himself — particularly not in a situation such as the party Williams describes in the *Times* piece in which he is talking to people who have presumably seen his work. Still, to write about "life" implies the looking at it and to see it from a particular pair of eyes hooked into a particular brain involves a personal way of seeing, a vision of life. By the time the vision is embedded in a plot, made ambulatory through characters, verbalized in lines that are to be spoken by actors on a stage — by the time it has been transmuted into a play — it has become an artistic vision and that means that themes, implicit and explicit, are walking abroad. What Williams probably means in the lines quoted above is that he does not set out to demonstrate an idea or to deliver a message in his plays. Even if we accept that as true (and we probably cannot do so for his later plays — *The Night of the Iguana, The Milk Train Doesn't Stop Here Anymore*), we must recognize that his choice of character and situation provides him with recurrent themes that turn up in his work from the earliest one-acters to *Milk Train*. A caveat: although Williams' plays all bear a family resemblance, each of them is an individual with its private strengths and weaknesses. There is no room in a work this short to do extensive analyses of his plays. In reading the discussion below of Williams' subject matter and his dramatic technique, it is well to remember that my somewhat generalized comments are only useful when they have been tried on a particular play and altered until they fit.

In 1950, Williams wrote an introduction to the New Classics Edition of Carson McCullers' novel *Reflections in a Golden Eye* in which he seems to be talking about himself as much as Mrs. McCullers. "It appears to me, sometimes, that there are only two kinds of people who live outside what E. E. Cummings has defined as 'this socalled world of ours' — the artists and the insane," he says and then he amends, "Of course there are those who are not practising artists and those who have not been committed to asylums, but who have enough of one or both magical elements, lunacy and vision, to permit them also to slip sufficiently apart from 'this socalled world of ours' to undertake or accept an exterior view of it." This is a rough definition of the kind of person who becomes the hero (or the heroine) of the Williams plays. The same kind of person usually fills a number of the minor roles and, in some of the plays, even acts as villain. What Williams is preoccupied with is not the artist or the insane, as such, but the man or woman who by virtue of being different can (in fact, must) stand outside and see the world clearly — which, for Williams, means to see the horror in it. Although many of his characters are artists or pseudo-artists and most of them are at least a little neurotic, a more general description of the Williams outsider is needed. Perhaps it can be found in *The Eccentricities of a Nightingale*, in which the word *eccentric* is used by the less sensitive characters as an accusatory label; in that play, Alma describes the literary club to which she belongs as "my little company of the faded and frightened and difficult and odd and lonely." The club scene is presented satirically (as it is in *Summer and Smoke*), but Williams has always recognized that his outsiders (from Amanda in *The Glass Menagerie* to Mrs. Goforth in *Milk Train*) are — from one angle, at least — comic characters. The laughter in them and at them need not detract from their other qualities, made all the stronger by their separateness — their courage, say, or their dignity. At the end of *The Glass Menagerie*, describing the dumb show that goes on while Tom speaks his last monologue, Williams says of Amanda: "Now that we cannot hear the mother's speech, her silliness is gone and she has dignity and tragic beauty."

In an earlier description of Williams' work (in *American Drama since World War II*), I used the label *fugitive kind* to cover all his artist-eccentrics. It still seems the most appropriate. Williams not only used the phrase as title for an early play of his, but he apparently acquiesced in its reuse as title to the movie version of *Orpheus Descending*. In *Battle of Angels*, Sandra uses the phrase to describe herself and Val, uses it too narrowly since it should be taken as a synonym of that other good label — *the dispossessed* — which Val, in the same play, uses to describe himself and Loon, the guitar-playing Negro vagrant whom he befriends. Within the generalized term, however, there are a variety of types. It might be useful to consider the variations of the fugitive within the kind — beginning with the two categories which Williams put forward in the McCullers essay:

1. The artist. A Williams artist need never put a word to paper or paint to canvas, for it is his temperament, his inclination, that defines him. When Harold Clurman, in *Lies Like Truth*, says of Blanche in *Streetcar*, "She is a poet, even if we are dubious about her understanding of the writers she names," he is describing the artist as Williams uses him. Williams may present him seriously (as in the ponderous Val in *Battle of Angels*, writing "The Book") or satirically (as in Sebastian in *Suddenly Last Summer*, producing one poem a year after a nine-month gestation period), but whether he is serious or comic, he is a man whose special sensibility keeps him from seeing the world through its own

18

eyes. The Williams artists form a large company. In *The Glass Menagerie*, Tom is trying to be a poet, and so is Matilda in *You Touched Me!* In *Summer and Smoke*, Alma, "The Nightingale of the Delta," sings and teaches singing and meets regularly with her bizarre literary society. Byron wanders through *Camino Real*. In *Orpheus Descending*, having put aside "The Book" to take up Loon's guitar, Val is still the central artist, although Vee Talbott, the visionary painter, shares the stage with him. Alexandra in *Sweet Bird of Youth*, like the heroine of *The Roman Spring of Mrs. Stone*, is a fading actress and Chance Wayne is an ex-chorus boy. In *The Night of the Iguana*, Hannah Jelkes, the artist, and her grandfather, "the world's oldest living and practicing poet," earn their way by making sketches or reciting in hotel dining rooms, thus managing to play both sides of the street which academic definition runs between the fine and the performing arts. Chris Flanders in *Milk Train* is a poet and a maker of mobiles and even Mrs. Goforth is a writer of sorts since she spends her last hours dictating her autobiography. To this group should probably be added Brick Pollitt of *Cat on a Hot Tin Roof*, for as an athlete he is a kind of artist, allied, in terms of his diminishing powers, to the aging actresses mentioned above. On these grounds, even Jim O'Connor, the gentleman caller of *Menagerie*, might be included, for he was a basketball star in high school; he had also sung the lead in the school production of *The Pirates of Penzance*.

2. The insane. As Williams uses the word in the McCullers essay, it is a positive restatement of the old bromide about the kinship of the poet and the madman. It is a dangerous category to try to define in Williams' plays because as soon as the label *insanity* is put on a character, part of the audience (including a number of critics) will back away from the play, muttering an incantatory word — the general *sick* or the precise *atypical* — which

disassociates them from what is going on on stage. A more gen-
teel word — *disturbed*, perhaps — might go down more easily.
Yet, Blanche is carried off to an asylum at the end of *Streetcar*
and Catharine, who may or may not be sane, is in an institution
in *Suddenly Last Summer*. Shannon has to be tied down in
Iguana and Hannah, who comforts him, hints of a dark night in
her own soul. The heroine of *Baby Doll* appears a little feeble-
minded, at least for most of the movie, and at the end of that
film Archie Lee has plainly run mad. Williams' plays offer a
gallery of hysterics, all little sisters to Blanche, ranging from Alma
in *Summer and Smoke* and Lady in *Orpheus*, both desperate for
the pills that will calm them, to poor Isabel in *Period of Adjustment*, who has to make do with Pepto-Bismol to settle her stom-
ach. Although Williams occasionally goes clinical, at least to the
extent of identifying Blanche as a "neurasthenic personality," he
more often works on a metaphorical level. Think of Alexandra
in the first act of *Sweet Bird*, swimming up out of sleep, crying for
her oxygen tank; in a scene that is both horrifying and very funny, Williams offers an image of the man who cannot catch his
breath in a world that is smothering him.

3. The cripple. This is a group which might comfortably take
in the characters discussed above as "insane." It is difficult to find
the line between mental and physical disturbances in a Williams
character. Is Laura in *Menagerie* crippled by her limp or her shy-
ness? Is George's tremor in *Period of Adjustment* in his head or in
his hands? It hardly matters really since the diseases, the injuries,
are as much metaphorical as they are real. Brick's broken ankle in
Cat, Kilroy's weak heart in *Camino Real*, Mrs. Venable's stroke in
Suddenly Last Summer, and the fatal cancer of Jabe in *Orpheus*,
Big Daddy in *Cat*, and Mrs. Goforth in *Milk Train* are all devices
that help indicate that they are special characters.

4. The sexual specialist. This is a hard category to put a label

ican writers, their absence is a bit odd. It is the missing Negro
most demands explanation since a view of the world which
the Mississippi delta country as its microcosm would seem to h
the Negro ready-made as an image of the fugitive kind. Exc
for Loon in *Battle of Angels*, the actual Negroes that appeal
Williams' plays — the neighbor woman in *Streetcar*, the maid
Period of Adjustment — hardly fit this image. Williams does
the image, but by analogy. His white characters on stage recogi
themselves in Negroes whom we hear about but never see. Th
Val in *Orpheus* identifies with the runaway convict (presuma
Negro) torn apart by dogs and Chance Wayne in *Sweet Bird* f
himself menaced by the kind of envy that caused a Negro to
taken at random and castrated. I do not presume to know whe
er this substitution arises from a psychological defense of W
liams', an artistic decision about audience identification, a gu
at what the Broadway market would take, or a combination of
three possibilities.

As the examples multiply in the categories above it becon
clear that the concept of the outsider, the fugitive kind, is on t
point of evaporating, of becoming a statement about human b
ings in general. After all, the list includes characters such as Ji
O'Connor, whose ideas are used in opposition to those of Tor
the more conventional Williams fugitive, and such as Jabe an
Miss Fellowes, who function as villains in their plays. If the ou
siders get too numerous, there will be no insiders to oppose them
In a sense, this is what Williams has begun to suggest in hi
more recent work. In "The World I Live In," an article for the
Observer, in which he interviews himself, he says of people in
general: "Well, I've never met one that I couldn't love if I completely knew him and understood him." Although the remark
sounds both pious and folksy, a cross between "to know all is to for-
give all" and Will Rogers' "I never met a man I didn't like," it

on because it has to take in such disparate characters. It
the virgins waiting to be initiated (Matilda in *You 1
Me!,* Alma in *Summer and Smoke,* Rosa and Jack in *Th
Tattoo,* George and Isabel in *Period of Adjustment*) and
who will not be (Laura in *Menagerie,* Hannah in *Iguana*),
who have chosen chastity to escape corruption (Val in *Or₁
Brick in *Cat*); the professionals and those amateurs so tal
they could go professional (Val, Stanley in *Streetcar,* Ch
Wayne in *Sweet Bird,* Camille and Casanova in *Camino R
the homosexuals, explicit (Charlus in *Camino,* Sebastian in *!
denly Last Summer,* Miss Fellowes in *Iguana*) and impl
(Brick); those with a desperate need for sex as a stimulant or
punishment (Blanche in *Streetcar,* Maggie in *Cat,* Carol in *C
pheus,* Alexandra in *Sweet Bird*). The thing that they all have i
common is an extreme sensitivity.

5. The foreigner. Two things are at work here: a fact and a
myth. It is a fact of American society — at least of the small-town
southern society into which Williams was born — that the foreigner, even when he ceases to be foreign, is an outsider. It is a
myth, one from northern Europe that was passed on to the United
States, that the Mediterranean peoples live richer, wilder, more
open lives than the cold, closed northerners. Thus we have Rosa
Gonzales and her father, the fiery Mexicans of *Summer and
Smoke;* the wild Sicilians of *The Rose Tattoo;* the corruption of
Camino Real which, according to a Williams stage direction, re-
calls Tangiers, Havana, Vera Cruz, Casablanca, Shanghai, and
New Orleans; the Italian Lady of *Orpheus;* the Sicilian with the
riding crop of *27 Wagons Full of Cotton,* softened a little for
Baby Doll; the Lorca-like setting for the offstage cannibalism of
Suddenly Last Summer; and the hot-blooded Mexican boys of
Iguana. There are no Jews (except for some offstage names) and
very few Negroes. Because these are the favorite outsiders of Amer-

contains the bridge between the outsider and the insider in the Williams plays. The insider is the man who is protected, by insensitivity or by a strong identification with the dominant group and its conventions, from knowledge of himself and the terrors around him; the outsider is the man who, by virtue of his strangeness, is particularly sensitive to horror. Williams is attracted to the second group and it is to them that he directs the sympathy of his audience.

His attitude toward the comfortable insiders has changed over the years, however; at least his fugitive kind no longer treat the others with an indifference that is a kind of contempt (as Tom did in *Menagerie*) or with open anger (as in the story "Two on a Party," in which the leading characters "loathed and despised" the "squares of the world"). It is true that Shannon in *Iguana* is still shouting out against the world that will not see what he sees (the world as a pile of excrement), but Hannah, in declaring her allegiance to him, speaks a gentle, even a pitying word for the others. "I respect a person that has had to fight and howl for his decency and his — " she begins and, then, after his interruption: "Yes, for his decency and his bit of goodness, much more than I respect the lucky ones that just had theirs handed out to them at birth and never afterwards snatched away from them by . . . unbearable . . . torments . . ." The implication of Hannah's speech is that only the degree of perception (a matter of luck) separates Shannon from the vacationing schoolteachers whom he despises. If the fine line between the outsiders and the insiders is barely kept intact in *Iguana*, it is broken in *Sweet Bird* when Chance speaks directly to the audience, asking for "your recognition of me in you."

In *Period of Adjustment* — perhaps because he chose to write something approximating a standard Broadway marriage comedy — Williams made an attempt to create characters who displayed all the clichés of imperceptive, ordinary people and to afflict them with the desperation of the fugitive kind. It is through this play — the least typical in the Williams canon — that the playwright indicates most clearly that what he has been talking about all along is not simply the special pain of an eccentric out-group but the human condition as he sees it.

If Williams' (man)kind is fugitive, then something has to be in pursuit. His characters are menaced by three things: by other people, by themselves, and by the universe. At one level, the first of these provides whatever social comment the Williams plays contain. This can be no more than casual satire aimed at the images of what passes for the "good life" in America — the deep freeze (Serafina's remarks in *The Rose Tattoo*) and the television-liquor cabinet (the stage directions in *Cat*). It is in *Period of Adjustment*, with its " 'cute' little Spanish-type suburban bungalow" built in a development that is slowly sinking into the ground ("High Point over a Cavern" is the play's subtitle), that Williams' use of this kind of satire is most extensive and most conventional. Except when they "carry the banner of Bohemia" (Casanova's line from *Camino*), the Williams characters are ambivalent about American materialism and its implications. Serafina both wants a deep freeze and uses it to denounce the cold American women who do not know love as she presumably does. Amanda insists that she has remarkable children "just *full* of natural endowments," but the insistence, insofar as she believes it, is as blatant an acceptance of the American success myth as Willy Loman's in *Death of a Salesman*. Lady in *Orpheus* wants to use the confectionery, which she has decorated to suggest her father's wine garden, as an attack on those (including her husband) who killed her father and as a means to conventional success. If the trappings of American success are dangerous, they are so not because they provide an alien threat but a corruption toward which the characters yearn. The danger is shown most clearly in plays such as *Menagerie*, in which Tom must escape not only the shoe warehouse but Amanda's demands which tie him to it; *Orpheus*, in which Val, the wild one, almost becomes a shoe clerk; *Period*, in which Ralph contemplates his situation and moans: *"oh, I wish I could be the first man in a moon rocket!"*

At this level, the social comment is relatively commonplace. It is a depiction of American success and its material attributes as empty and ludicrous. In other instances, Williams' comments become much harsher, dig under the surface to turn up the avariciousness and fear that presumably motivate those who want to find and hold their place in the "good life." While Brick and Big Daddy act out their drama of truth and mendacity in *Cat*, they are surrounded by characters who want to get their hands on Big Daddy's money, from the nattering clergyman who cannot quit talking about memorial windows to Mae and Gooper, who try to use their "no-neck monsters" as pawns in the inheritance game; even Maggie, a spitting cat on a hot tin roof, fears deprivation of money as much as she suffers deprivation of sex. Mrs. Holly and George in *Suddenly Last Summer*, loyal and lovely family types, seem willing to trade Catharine's frontal lobe for the inheritance from Sebastian. Although these characters might be taken simply as greedy individuals, the implication is that they represent the society in which they live and function. In at least three of the Williams works — *Orpheus, Sweet Bird*, and *Baby Doll* — the playwright places his characters in a context that is political as well as social, that provides an implied attack on the self-protective nastiness (of which racism is a manifestation) that burns Val, castrates Chance, endangers Silva.

Although the social commentary here is often direct (in the revised version of *Orpheus*, one of Val's lynchers stops to rob the till), and is certainly genuine, it is finally secondary. Even Boss

Finley, who holds a whole state in his control in *Sweet Bird,* is
— in his political guise — only a symptom. It is the evil spirits
abroad in the world that Williams wants to depict. Silva in *Baby
Doll* explains what they are: "Spirits of violence — and cunning
— malevolence — cruelty — treachery — destruction. . . ." Baby
Doll, who is not always as simple as she is supposed to be, answers, "Oh, them's just human characteristics." The destructive
cruelty that dogs the fugitive kind, then, may be social and political on occasion, but it is always human. Sometimes, it is in-
cidental — a character like the traveling salesman who wanders
through *The Rose Tattoo,* stopping just long enough to knee
Alvaro in the groin. More often — particularly in the plays in
which the outsider is to be destroyed — it is embodied in a central character — Boss Finley, for instance, or Jabe in *Orpheus* —
and repeated in peripheral figures — Tom, Jr., and Chance's old
school chums in *Sweet Bird,* Dog and Pee Wee in *Orpheus.*

The classic example, of course, is Stanley in *A Streetcar Named
Desire,* the insensitive brute who drives Blanche to destruction.
He would be such an example, that is, if we took Williams'
word for what the play is about: "The rape of Blanche by Stanley
is a pivotal, integral truth in the play, without which the play
loses its meaning, which is the ravishment of the tender, the sensitive, the delicate, by the savage and brutal forces of modern
society." The quotation is from a letter Williams wrote to Joseph
I. Breen, the chief censor for the Production Code, making a plea
to retain the integrity of the movie version of *Streetcar.* Under
such circumstances, he might be expected to overstate his case. Although Williams' sympathy plainly goes out to Blanche, *Streetcar* is too balanced a play to let her operate simply as a sensitive
victim. From her first appearance, when preoccupied with her own
fatigue and pain she insults the amiable Eunice, Blanche is, as
Williams once called her, "a delicate tigress with her back to the

wall." Her destructiveness is clear both in the immediate action on stage (her disruption of Stella's marriage) and in the expositional past (her attack on her husband Allan). In Blanche's descent into madness, we can see one of Williams' outsiders broken by one of the "others," but in much of her behavior we can see that she, too, is an "other" and that Stanley is in danger of becoming a victim.

This ambiguous sense of who is the victim and who the victimizer is used extensively in the later plays in which, to use the metaphor provided by *Suddenly Last Summer*, the eaters sometimes become the eaten. *Sweet Bird*, for all its confusion, offers one of the clearest statements of this. Both Alexandra and Chance are victims within the wide context of the play, but within the terms of their relationship they keep changing the roles of destroyer and destroyed. She describes him as "Lost in the beanstalk country, the ogre's country at the top of the beanstalk, the country of the flesh-hungry, blood-thirsty ogre" and she begs him not to leave her: "If you do I'll turn into the monster again. I'll be the first lady of the Beanstalk Country." He calls her "nice monster" and she calls him "pitiful monster." Both are amateur monsters compared to Boss Finley, but Williams plainly intends that that character should be more than caricature, that he too should be monster-ridden. That he does not come across that way is one of the artistic failures of the play, as Williams himself admitted when he said of Boss Finley's scene, "The act is weak because I couldn't really identify with Boss Finley." Couldn't, to use the terminology from the *Observer* piece quoted above, come to love him. In the revised *Sweet Bird*, Boss Finley — still unloved apparently — has almost disappeared, is given no more than a line or two to bring down an act curtain.

Although the Williams characters are constantly hurt and harried by those around them, they are also tortured by something

27

within themselves — guilt and fear primarily/ Tom in *Menagerie*, guilty at deserting Laura, can no more escape the memory of her than Blanche, guilty at having driven Allan to suicide, can stop the accusing polka music from pounding in her head. Brick in *Cat* waits for the click in his head which will turn off his suspicion that he is responsible for his friend Skipper's death. Fear cripples Laura in *Menagerie*, almost immobilizes Matilda in *You Touched Me!*, gives to George in *Period* a physical tremor. The fear here is of failure — sexual in George's case — which causes a withdrawal, a defense against the possibility of being hurt. A more important kind of fear in Williams' work is that of Alexandra in *Sweet Bird* (fear of growing old) and of Mrs. Goforth in *Milk Train* (fear of death) and with this concept of fear we get to the third and most menacing of the pursuers in the Williams plays.

That pursuer may be called the universe, or human mortality, or the absence of God, but Williams most often uses the label with which Chance ends *Sweet Bird* — "the enemy, time, in us all." An early version of that play, a one-acter, is called *The Enemy: Time*. From *Menagerie* on, time has been chasing the Williams characters. Amanda states the implacable fact when she warns Tom "that the future becomes the present, the present the past, and the past turns into everlasting regret if you don't plan for it," and Williams echoes her words in an introduction he wrote for the New Classics Edition of that play, "the monosyllable of the clock is Loss, loss, loss, unless you devote your heart to its opposition." In both these statements, there is the suggestion that time can be outmaneuvered or neutralized by some kind of activity. It is a young man's statement, one which Williams seems never to have believed. His plays are full of characters — Blanche, Marguerite in *Camino*, Alexandra, and Chance — whom the loss has made desperate. Although Wil-

28

liams likes to use fading beauties and aging athletes as his time-consumed characters, it is clear that it is not simply the loss of youth and beauty that preoccupies him. It is the fact of death. This can be seen in Big Daddy in *Cat* and Mrs. Goforth in *Milk Train*, both of whom try to pretend that they are not dying, and even more clearly in Jabe in *Orpheus*, a death figure who uses destruction in a vain attempt to hang onto life. Williams' conception of man is of one dogged by the knowledge of death and, hence, scarcely able to live the little life he has.

In several of his recent plays — noticeably *Suddenly Last Summer* and *Iguana* — Williams has been considering the nature of the universe in a specific manner, but it is the universe that has been implicit in all his work, one in which man is a stranger and can find comfort, if at all, only in himself and his own kind. In *Suddenly Last Summer*, there are conflicting views of God, neither designed to bring peace to the troubled soul. Sebastian imagines that he has seen God in watching the flesh-eating birds destroy the baby turtles and, acting on that vision, he allows himself to be so destroyed. Dr. Sugar, who says that "doctors look for God, too," offers a vision which is even more horrifying, for it is described in soft and human words: the blue sky, free of Sebastian's birds, which cannot be seen until the looker has had a lobotomy. Shannon in *Iguana* shares Sebastian's cruel God, but that play makes specific what *Suddenly* only implies, that the universe is in fact an impersonal thing and that the Gods of Sebastian, of Sugar, of Shannon are all created in their own images. This is made clear in *Iguana* when the titular animal is likened to human beings ("At the end of its rope") and when Shannon goes to cut it loose, to play God "because God won't do it."

There is no escape in a universe where there is no God and where the other inhabitants are as dangerous as one's own self. In *Orpheus*, the conjure man offers Carol a charm, the breastbone of a bird, which she rejects because it "isn't clean yet, there's still some flesh clinging to it," because until "every sign of corruption is burned and washed away" it is not a good charm; at the end, she accepts Val's snakeskin jacket, for it is clean. Val has escaped into death. His sacrifice (he is both Orpheus and Christ) has meaning, for he has passed on to Carol the possibility of a spirit in man which lifts him out of the cruelty, the jealousy, the despair that has killed Lady and lynched the savior (Val Xavier). Here — as in *Camino Real*, in which Kilroy and Don Quixote set out for the mountains where the violets have at last broken the rocks — Williams is at his most romantic, offering the fugitive kind as a company of the elect. Most of the time, however, there are no romantic solutions. At best, the characters make do.

There are two main ways of trying to escape in the Williams plays. The first of these is by running. Williams once published an article in the *New York Times Magazine*, "A Writer's Quest for a Parnassus," which was not quite the innocent travel piece that it seemed to be. In it, he says that a writer — particularly an American writer — has to keep moving, trying to find the place in which he can feel at home, in which he can write. Williams' characters are as mobile as he is. Tom in *Menagerie* attempts "to find in motion what was lost in space." Blanche comes to New Orleans in search of sanctuary, if not Parnassus, and is about to move on when Stanley's rape brings an end to her running. Val is a wanderer in *Orpheus* and Carol is forever heading somewhere (or nowhere) in that car of hers. Sebastian is described in *Suddenly* as an unrelenting traveler. Alexandra and Chance in *Sweet Bird* break a cross-country drive and find horror in St. Cloud. George and Isabel are on a honeymoon trip in *Period*. A group of wanderers gather at Maxine's in *Iguana* and some of them — Nonno and Shannon, perhaps — come to rest. With the possible exception of Shannon, all of these characters either keep moving or are stopped by death or disaster. Running never frees any of them from the pursuer.

The second attempt to escape is hardly that really. It is more properly a temporary surcease, a little comfort found along the road. At the end of *Menagerie*, Tom speaks of walking in a strange city, "before I have found companions." Tom's temporary companions, the lovers that Blanche or Carol finds, Sebastian's young men, Alexandra's gigolos, Mrs. Goforth's husbands — all these are images of attempts at human contact, "one night stands" as Shannon calls them in *Iguana*. In *Camino Real*, we hear Marguerite (Camille) playing a "love" scene with Casanova, two romantics down on their luck in a world for which *down-on-your-luck* is a descriptive term: "we stretch out hands to each other in the dark that we can't escape from — we huddle together for some dim-communal comfort." In *Milk Train*, Christopher has a long metaphorical speech in which he describes men as kittens or puppies, "living in a house we're not used to," creeping close together — "those gentle little nudges with our paws and our muzzles" — to find in contact some escape from fear. In only two of the Williams plays is there a suggestion of a conventional happy ending, of a love that is more than a momentary rest — *You Touched Me!*, in which Hadrian rescues Matilda from spinsterdom, and *The Rose Tattoo*, in which Serafina marches out to Alvaro shouting, "Vengo, vengo, amore!" Unhappy extenuating circumstances might be found to explain away the apparent endings of these two plays. Certainly Williams' most conventional happy ending — that of *Period of Adjustment* — is most unconventional. In the standard Broadway marriage comedy the complications are straightened out, which is to say glossed over, by sending the hero and heroine to bed. In his "serious comedy," Williams sends not one, but two couples to bed and just as they are about to cuddle into the familiar final curtain, there is a cracking noise as the house sinks a little farther into the cavern over which it is built; the conventional ending then follows, but it, like the house, is now a little awry. Surely, Williams, who uses sexual imagery casually, comically in all his plays, is punning on his subtitle; "High Point over a Cavern" suggests not only moving in for the sex act, but the diversion itself over the grave. In any case, the play gets the same image elsewhere: George and Isabel are on their honeymoon, driving a funeral limousine.

In the most recent Williams plays, the sense of desperation has begun to disappear, to be replaced by a kind of acceptance. Perhaps this quality can be found in *The Eccentricities of a Nightingale*, in which Albertine's button becomes the central metaphor for Alma's one night with John. Alma tells him the story of her aunt's unsuitable but happy marriage and of how Albertine, trying to save her husband from a burning building, stumbled out of the fire, clutching the button that pulled from his jacket, and died saying, "Some people . . . don't even die empty-handed!" That play, however, is difficult to date. I am thinking primarily of *Iguana* and *Milk Train*, both unusual Williams plays in that each of them involves two leading characters who do not join physically. One of the two in each case acts as a kind of spiritual guide. Hannah teaches Shannon to accept life and Chris teaches Mrs. Goforth to accept death; it is the same lesson. This apparent new calm may, of course, be temporary; wherever Williams' road takes him from here it is likely — on the evidence of his first twenty years as a playwright — that he will be coming again (from whatever angle) at the themes that have so long obsessed him.

From the beginning of his career, Williams has been trying to tell the *real* truth (his real truth, that is) about human beings and the way they live, but he has never wanted to do that as a realist. He has made constant use of both literary and theatrical devices of a nonrealistic sort because, as he insists in the Production Notes to *The Glass Menagerie*, "truth, life, or reality is an organic thing which the poetic imagination can represent or suggest, in essence, only through transformation, through changing into other forms than those which were merely present in appearance." His use of devices ranges from the subtle to the shockingly obvious, from organic machine to pure gimmick. Williams at his most gimmicky can be seen in the screen device of *Menagerie* and in the stage assistants of *The Milk Train Doesn't Stop Here Anymore*. For *Menagerie*, he suggests that words or pictures be flashed on a screen, verbal or visual comments which, if we can believe his justification published with the play, he intends as guides to an obtuse audience, explaining each scene and its relation to the whole. Unless his purpose in *Menagerie* is to mock his characters (which hardly seems likely), his device would be a failure, for the screened comments seem designed to reduce all the scenes — even the tenderest — to ludicrous parodies. For instance, in the dinner scene, when Laura, panic-stricken at the idea of sitting down with the gentleman caller, drags herself unwillingly toward the table, Williams calls for this legend: "TERROR!" As she stumbles and Amanda and Tom cry out, the screen says, "AH!" This would put us back with the Gish sisters in the silent movies and not, as the device suggests, with Piscator and Brecht on the edge of the Epic Theater. I use the "would" purposely because Eddie Dowling discarded the screen device in the original production of *Menagerie*, a practice since followed extensively; yet, Williams cares enough for the device to retain it in the published version of the play. In *Milk Train*, he introduces two stage assistants whose double job is to comment on what happens and to direct the point of action by removing a screen from in front of whatever playing area is to be used; since the play does not need their comments (as the Yeats plays do those of similar figures) and since lighting could spot the action, they remain arty intrusions, made foolish by Williams' distrust of the audience, which forces these non-characters to use the first scene to explain who and what they are.

If *Menagerie* is one extreme of Williams' antirealism, it also contains examples of his use of realistic technique. Despite his aesthetic stand, he is enough in the tradition of the American theater to ask his characters to move and speak realistically when he wants them to. Consider, for example, the opening of the second scene of *Menagerie* in which Amanda comes home, having discovered that Laura has dropped out of business college. Her accusation begins before she starts to speak, is apparent in the air of martyrdom with which she slowly removes her hat and gloves, drops them to the floor, digs in her purse for a handkerchief, touches it to her lips. Williams calls all this "a bit of acting," but, although the gestures are overelaborate, the scene is realistic because they are Amanda's gestures not Williams'. *Menagerie* provides Tom with the ornate and rather trying "poetic" monologue which opens the play, but at the same time it gives him a fine quarrel scene with Amanda in which both speech and action are realistic. The realistic element never disappears from the Williams plays. As late as *Iguana*, we see character-defining action, as in the scene in Act II in which Maxine tempts Shannon with the rum-coco; as late as *Period of Adjustment*, we see character-revealing speech, as in Isabel's story of her dream of serving with a handsome doctor, during which, as it becomes more clearly a movie plot, she suddenly shifts from the first to the third person. Although Williams does not write psychological drama in the conventional sense — Jim's analysis of Laura in *Menagerie* is both accurate and irrelevant, a joke about pat labels — he is psychologically sound in his choice of gesture and word. That I suppose is a way of saying that he can create character when he wants to, can put real frogs in his imaginary gardens.

Realism of a kind, then, lies at the core of his talent for creating characters (probably his greatest talent), but it would be unfair to his work to dwell heavily on that element in it. After all, he has done his best to mask it. He has used caricature extensively, sometimes in terms of Broadway convention (the clergyman in *Cat*, the businessman-father in *Period*), but more often in terms of other traditions of the theater. He calls Flora and Bessie in *The Rose Tattoo* "two female clowns" and describes them in terms of physical contrast — "tall and angular" and "rather stubby." This is the Laurel-and-Hardy bit, a standard comic contrast that circuses and music halls have found funny for years; perhaps recognizing that Bessie and Flora constituted a comic turn, Williams gave them a one-acter of their own, *A Perfect Analysis Given by a Parrot* (1958). Comic caricature of another kind can be found in characters such as Alexandra in *Sweet Bird* and Archie Lee in *Baby Doll*, grotesques which suggest Ben Jonson; surely if Jonson had ever thought to do a self-deluding lesbian whose repressions had turned her into a Puritan hatchet man, he would have come up with a Zeal-of-the-hand Busy like Miss Fellowes in *Iguana*. Williams is not writing Jonsonian satire, of course; he is using his grotesques to express a condition that is at once horrible and comic.

Williams has many devices other than caricature to lift his characters out of the realistic tradition. He uses mythic identifications, for instance, as in *Orpheus*, in which Val is the titular singer, and in *Suddenly*, in which Sebastian suggests the saint of the same name; both of these characters, as well as Chance and Boss Finley in *Sweet Bird*, Shannon in *Iguana*, and Christopher in *Milk Train*, are identified by the audience or by one of the other characters as Christ figures. In *Camino Real*, the characters are borrowed directly from literature (Camille, Charlus, Don Quixote), from life (Casanova, Byron), from popular usage (Kilroy), or they are given significant names (A. Ratt, Gutman). The use of significant names is one of Williams' favorite games. Sometimes they are used realistically, as in *Streetcar* and *Summer and Smoke*, in which the characters themselves point out that Blanche DuBois is white woods, Stella is star, Alma is soul. More often Williams uses the device himself, often comically, as in Chance Wayne, whose chances have waned, and in George Haverstick, who, through sexual fear, may be said to have no stick at all.

Mythic identifications and significant names are literary ways of stressing the nonrealistic element in character; there are theatrical means that work as well. In *Streetcar*, for instance, the nurse and the doctor are presented as ominous figures (like the nun in *Suddenly*), institutional extensions rather than individuals; when the doctor removes his hat, just before he offers Blanche his arm, Williams says "he becomes personalized." Such depersonalization can only be used with peripheral characters, but there are ways of establishing the artificiality, the theatricality of even the leading characters. The one that Williams uses most extensively is to present the long speeches as set pieces, arias almost, delivered to the audience rather than to other characters. Amanda's telephone speeches in *Menagerie* are early examples of this (Tom's soliloquies, being outside the action, are another matter), but it is in *Cat*, with Maggie's long speeches in the first act, that the device begins to take the form that it will have increasingly in the later plays. Brick is present, Maggie is presumably talking to him and he is even given occasional lines of comment, but the scene is, in fact, a kind of solo performance for the actress who plays Maggie. In the later plays, Williams stresses the special character of such speeches. Beulah's, at the beginning of *Orpheus*, should, so Williams tells us in the stage direction, "set the non-realistic key for the whole production." In *Suddenly*, Dr. Sugar leads Catharine to the forestage to describe her seduction and, when she explains what happened last summer, she is in a white spot while the other characters fade into the background. When Chance tells his story in *Sweet Bird*, he, too, moves to the forestage and when Alexandra does her telephone scene she opens it with lines that describe not only the position of the characters within the play but of the actors within the scene: "He's in the dimmed out background . . . I've taken the light again as a crown on my head . . ."

In *The Life of the Drama*, Eric Bentley suggests two rules for the beginning playwright: "if you wish to attract the audience's attention, be violent: if you wish to hold it, be violent again." Williams found those rules for himself long before Bentley put them into words. How one feels about Williams depends on the emphasis (the motivation, if you like) one puts on "to attract" and "to hold." It was fashionable for a while – particularly in the late 1950's when Williams turned out a string of violent plays, *Orpheus, Suddenly, Sweet Bird* – to assume that the playwright was simply venal, tickling a sick American audience where it was most vulnerable. There may be a touch of the mercenary in what Williams calls his "cornpone melodrama," but we must assume a touch of the poet as well. In his introduction to *Reflections in a Golden Eye*, he explains that art has not the room that life has, that "the awfulness has to be compressed," that the writer is driven to "symbols of the grotesque and the violent." Although any event in a Williams play is likely to have a counterpart somewhere in fact, his lurid plots are not intended to be realistic. They are what James Thurber, in another context, called "fables for our time."

If one describes *Orpheus Descending* flatly, it may be possible to imagine it as a realistic play: a young tramp arrives in a Mississippi town, goes to work in a shoe store, impregnates his boss while her husband lies dying upstairs, and is burned to death by a gang of lynchers, spurred on by the husband who has stayed alive long enough to shoot his wife to death. In these terms, *Orpheus* would be simply a melodrama of lust and murder. Williams takes great pains to keep the audience from being hypnotized by the events of the play, from getting stuck at the realistic level. The mythic elements and the unrealistic staging — both mentioned in the paragraphs above on character — are ways of keeping an audience from taking the plot literally. It would be as well not to lean too far in the other direction, not to take the myth literally. It is amusing with the Williams plays to try to fit myth to plot — to see Orpheus (Val) with his lyre (guitar), descending into Hades (a small southern town) to rescue Eurydice (Lady) from Death (Jabe). Williams, however, does not work that neatly. His Val is identified not only with Orpheus (by the title and his guitar), but with Christ (through Vee Talbott's painting and his last name) and St. Valentine (through his first name). What Williams wants to do is to make Val's death — like Sebastian's death in *Suddenly* and Chance's castration in *Sweet Bird* — a kind of ritual that lifts the plot from the realistic to the metaphorical. The references to Greek and Christian myth that sprinkle his plays serve as distancing devices, pushing us away from a strictly realistic reading, even when they are used humorously — as with the Infant of Prague in *Period of Adjustment*.

The verbal and visual symbols that flood the Williams plays have much the same use. ". . . I have a poet's weakness for symbols," says Tom in *Menagerie*. It is a statement that Williams might well have printed on his own calling cards. Almost any Williams play could provide a plethora of symbols, but *Summer and Smoke* should give us enough to see the kind (and the qual-

ity) of symbols that he is capable of. To begin with, a stone an-
gel, called ETERNITY, broods over the action. In this presence, a
struggle between soul (Alma) and body (John) is acted out, one
which lets each recognize within himself what he has seen and
reached for in the other. The division is made clear through the
two main playing areas (the rectory and the doctor's office) and the
two points of view are made extremely explicit through Alma's
speech on the Gothic cathedral ("the everlasting struggle and as-
piration for more than our human limits have placed in our
reach") and John's lecture, using the anatomy chart, in which he
points out the brain, the belly, the sex, all of which must be fed.
John as sexual figure is emphasized in his first scene with Alma
when a Roman candle (seven puffs!) goes off behind them.
Alma's reaching-for-the-stars theme is echoed elsewhere in the
play, as in Scene 7 in which Gonzales, who has been playing
poker, uses the phrase "The sky is the limit" to indicate the way
he wants to lift his daughter Rosa from the dirt-floored house of
her childhood ("le doy el cielo!"); or in Scene 11, when John,
explaining that it is nothing physical in Alma he wants, strikes
a match and cups it until it flames upward. There is a running
business about a plumed hat. In Scene 1, John tells Alma to
wear one when she goes riding with him and she does wear one —
too late — when she comes to his office in Scene 11, ready to ad-
mit that she has been won over to his view. The plumed hat is
used also, and most effectively, in Scene 2 in the quarrel between
Alma and her mother in which the plume is torn loose in their
physical struggle.

There is a great deal too much going on symbolically in *Summer and Smoke* and all of it — from the ludicrous Roman candle
to the embarrassingly obvious anatomy chart to the dramatically
useful plumed hat — is presumably to be taken seriously. In oth
er Williams plays, however, the symbols are a little tongue-in-

cheek; in *The Rose Tattoo*, for instance, it must be a joke that both Serafina's husband and her lover are truck drivers who carry bananas. By making so many symbols and by overexplaining his main ones (as with the iguana in *Iguana*), Williams uses them to insist on the nonrealistic quality of the plays rather than (like Chekhov with his cherry orchard) intensifying whatever realism there is.

As though pushing his characters toward caricature and his plots toward myth and decorating both with symbols were not enough, Williams makes use of every possible tool of the theater — sets, props, lights, sound — to emphasize that his plays are not realistic. The schematic set demanded by the soul-body split of *Summer and Smoke* is typical of his work. The only play in which he ever called for a conventional set is *Period of Adjustment*, which is in part a joke on the conventions it is using, but even it has some unusual features. Ralph and Isabel do not play their almost love scene in front of a very real fireplace, as Candida and Marchbanks do in Shaw's play, but in front of "a flickering red light" set in the invisible fourth wall which puts the audience into the fireplace — a device Williams also uses in *The Eccentricities of a Nightingale*. For Williams, sets are not solid indications of his characters' environment, as they are for Ibsen and Shaw. They are suggestive of a mood, often with an empty sky (a theological comment?) hanging over the action. In the "Notes for the Designer" at the beginning of *Cat on a Hot Tin Roof* (in terms of action and character, one of Williams' most realistic plays), the playwright describes the setting, using the novelistic technique familiar in playwrights like Shaw, and then withdraws the realistic implications of his remarks: "I think the walls below the ceiling should dissolve mysteriously into air; the set should be roofed by the sky; stars and moon suggested by traces of milky pallor . . ." Perhaps the best indication of Williams' sense of what a scene on stage should look like (or feel like) is his ready use of painters and paintings to evoke a sense of the set: the lighting of *Menagerie* should suggest El Greco's religious paintings; the poker party in *Streetcar* recalls Van Gogh's billiard parlor; the fragmentary set walls of *Summer and Smoke* are out of Chirico; the porch and yard in *The Gnädiges Fräulein* are awry as though Picasso had designed them.

As with sets, so with props and costumes. The bed in *Cat*, "a functional part of the set," is raked to become a playing area itself; more than a bed — even a prop bed — it is a continual reminder of the struggle between Maggie and Brick. The mannequins in *The Rose Tattoo*, among which Williams calls for a bride and a widow, "who face each other in violent attitudes, as though having a shrill argument," are used not only to comment on Serafina's difficulties, but on occasion to harass her — as in Scene 5 where they seem to be interfering with her attempt to get to Rosa's graduation. Costumes in the early plays are often used to emphasize characters as in the white that Blanche wears ("that suggests a moth") or the primary colors of the men's shirts in the poker scene. Such use, of course, is not a departure from the realistic tradition. In the later plays, however, Williams often emphasizes costume as costume. The most obvious instance is in *The Night of the Iguana* in which Hannah puts on her artist's smock and Shannon his clericals, each in his own cubicle: "They are like two actors in a play which is about to fold on the road . . ." Later, Hannah puts on her Kabuki robe ("as an actor puts on a costume") and in *Milk Train* both Mrs. Goforth and Chris dress up in Kabuki robes.

Williams makes extensive use of sound and light for nonrealistic effects. In *Menagerie*, he calls for a musical theme which can be identified with Laura, and in *Streetcar*, the "Varsouviana," the polka that was playing when Allan shot himself, is used both to indicate and to intensify Blanche's desperation. Street cries ("Red hots!"; "Flores para los muertos") in that play are obviously more than local color. Uncle Pleasant's Choctaw call is used twice in *Orpheus* as entrance cues for Val, and bird cries are used antiphonally in several of the plays — most notably, *Suddenly Last Summer*. Williams has always demanded that his lighting do more than illumine the stage (it was the light that was to make an El Greco madonna of Laura); in the later plays, he has been using it not only for mood and character delineation, but also, as in *Sweet Bird* and *Suddenly*, to dim out the peripheral characters while a single one commands the audience's attention. Light can be used as a dramatic metaphor, as in *The Eccentricities of a Nightingale*, when the dead fireplace flames again, indicating that Alma and John can make love, and as a visual parallel, as in *Camino Real*, where the blue flame in the chafing dish on the Mulligans' table flares up and dies down while Marguerite and Jacques discuss dying in a sanitarium. Light and sound work together often — for instance, to create the symbolic storms that break over the Broadway version of *Cat* (Daddy's violent reaction to the news of approaching death, followed by his calm) and *Iguana* ("Here is your God, Mr. Shannon").

A random sampling, such as the one offered by the last few pages, can do no more than indicate the variety of literary and theatrical devices that Williams uses. What is clear is that a playwright who has a sharp eye for the nuances of speech and gesture which have always been of great importance to the realistic dramatist has consistently chosen to work in the nonrealistic tradition.

◣ Selected Bibliography

Works of Tennessee Williams

LONG PLAYS

The parenthetic dates represent the first New York production. Unless otherwise indicated, the multiple listings are for variant versions of the often rewritten plays. Works available from New American Library, New York, in paperback reprint editions are indicated (NAL) below.

Battle of Angels (1940). In *Pharos,* nos. 1–2 (Spring 1945). Also (with no change) in *Orpheus Descending with Battle of Angels.* New York: New Directions, 1958. Pp. 119–238.

The Glass Menagerie (1945). New York: Random House, 1945. New York: Dramatists Play Service, 1948.

You Touched Me! (1945), with Donald Windham. New York: Samuel French, 1947.

A Streetcar Named Desire (1947). New York: New Directions, 1947. (There are two versions of the play published under the same title page. The NAL reprint, $.50, is the second version.) New York: Dramatists Play Service, 1953.

Summer and Smoke (1948). New York: New Directions, 1948. (NAL, $.50.) New York: Dramatists Play Service, 1950.

The Rose Tattoo (1951). New York: New Directions, 1951. (NAL, $.35.)

Camino Real (1953). New York: New Directions, 1953. (Reprinted in paperback in *Famous American Plays of the 1950s,* edited by Lee Strasberg. New York: Dell. $.75.)

Cat on a Hot Tin Roof (1955). New York: New Directions, 1955. (NAL, $.50.) New York: Dramatists Play Service, 1958.

Baby Doll (1956). New York: New Directions, 1956. (NAL, $.35.) (Screenplay.)

Orpheus Descending (1957). In *Orpheus Descending with Battle of Angels.* New York: New Directions, 1958. Pp. 1–118. (NAL reprint titled *The Fugitive Kind,* $.35.) New York: Dramatists Play Service, 1959.

Suddenly Last Summer (1958). New York: New Directions, 1958. In *Garden District.* London: Secker and Warburg, 1959. Pp. 27–72. (NAL, $.50.)

Sweet Bird of Youth (1959). In *Esquire,* 51:114–55 (April 1959). New York: New Directions, 1959. (NAL, $.50.) New York: Dramatists Play Service, 1962.

Period of Adjustment (1960). In *Esquire,* 54:210–76 (December 1960). New

43

GERALD WEALES

York: New Directions, 1960. (NAL, $.50.) New York: Dramatists Play Service, 1961.

The Night of the Iguana (1961). In *Esquire*, 57:48–62, 115–30 (February 1962). New York: New Directions, 1962. (NAL, $.50.) New York: Dramatists Play Service, 1963.

The Milk Train Doesn't Stop Here Anymore (1964). New York: New Directions, 1964.

The Eccentricities of a Nightingale. In *The Eccentricities of a Nightingale and Summer and Smoke*. New York: New Directions, 1965. Pp. 1–107.

Slapstick Tragedy, Two Plays. In *Esquire*, 64:95–102, 130–34 (August 1965). (*The Mutilated* and *The Gnädiges Fräulein*, which, Williams says in his Production Notes, "should be performed together.")

SHORT PLAYS

American Blues: Five Short Plays. New York: Dramatists Play Service, 1948.

27 Wagons Full of Cotton and Other One-Act Plays. Norfolk, Conn.: New Directions, 1946, 1953. (The 1953 edition is most complete, with 13 plays.)

At Liberty. In *American Scenes*, edited by William Kozlenko. New York: John Day, 1941. Pp. 175–82.

I Rise in Flame, Cried the Phoenix. Norfolk, Conn.: New Directions, 1951.

Lord Byron's Love Letter. New York: Ricordi, 1955. (Libretto for a one-act opera by Raffaello de Banfield; it differs from the play in *27 Wagons*.)

A Perfect Analysis Given by a Parrot. New York: Dramatists Play Service, 1958.

The Enemy: Time. In *Theatre*, 1:14–17 (March 1959).

FICTION AND POETRY

The Roman Spring of Mrs. Stone. New York: New Directions, 1950. (NAL, $.50.) (Novel.)

One Arm, and Other Stories. New York: New Directions, 1948, reprinted 1954.

Hard Candy, a Book of Stories. New York: New Directions, 1954, reprinted 1959.

"Man Bring This Up Road." In *Mademoiselle*, 49:56–61, 102 (July 1959).

"The Summer Belvedere." In *Five Young Poets*, Third Series. Norfolk, Conn.: New Directions, 1944. Pp. 121–70.

In the Winter of Cities. New York: New Directions, 1956. (Poetry. The 1964 paperback edition, $1.50, is the most complete edition.)

ESSAYS

Introductory essays also appear in a number of the volumes listed above.

"The Catastrophe of Success." In *New York Times*, November 30, 1947, Section 2, p. 1. Also in the New Classics Edition of *The Glass Menagerie.* New York: New Directions, 1949. Pp. xiii–xix.

"Questions without Answers." In *New York Times,* October 3, 1948, Section 2, pp. 1, 3.

"A Writer's Quest for a Parnassus." In *New York Times Magazine,* August 13, 1950, pp. 16, 35.

"This Book." Introduction to New Classics Edition of Carson McCullers, *Reflections in a Golden Eye.* New York: New Directions, 1950. Pp. ix–xxi.

"The Human Psyche — Alone." In *Saturday Review of Literature,* 33:19–20 (December 23, 1950).

"Facts about Me" (1952). Record Cover, Caedmon TC 100.

"Critic Says 'Evasion,' Writer Says 'Mystery.' " In *New York Herald Tribune,* April 17, 1955, Section 4, pp. 1, 2.

"The World I Live In." In *Observer,* April 7, 1957, p. 14. Also in *Drama on Stage,* edited by Randolph Goodman. New York: Holt, Rinehart, and Winston, 1961. Pp. 293–95.

"Author and Director: A Delicate Situation." In *Playbill,* 1:9–13 (September 30, 1957).

Introduction to William Inge, *The Dark at the Top of the Stairs.* New York: Random House, 1958. Pp. vii–ix.

"Reflections on a Revival of a Controversial Fantasy." In *New York Times,* May 15, 1960, Section 2, pp. 1, 3.

"Tennessee Williams Presents His POV." In *New York Times Magazine,* June 12, 1960, pp. 19, 78.

"Prelude to a Comedy." In *New York Times,* November 6, 1960, Section 2, pp. 1, 3.

"The Agent as Catalyst." In *Esquire,* 58:216, 260 (December 1962).

"T. Williams's View of T. Bankhead." In *New York Times,* December 29, 1963, Section 2, pp. 1, 3.

Interviews

Funke, Lewis, and John E. Booth. "Williams on Williams," *Theatre Arts,* 46:17–19, 72–73 (January 1962).

Gelb, Arthur. "Williams and Kazan and the Big Walk-Out," *New York Times,* May 1, 1960, Section 2, pp. 1, 3.

"Man Named Tennessee," *Newsweek,* 49:81 (April 1, 1957).

Ross, Don. "Williams in Art and Morals," *New York Herald Tribune,* March 3, 1957, Section 4, pp. 1, 2.

Weatherby, W. J. "Lonely in Uptown New York," *Manchester Guardian Weekly,* 81:14 (July 23, 1959).

Biography and Criticism

Falk, Signi Lenea. *Tennessee Williams*. New York: Twayne, 1961. (Contains a descriptive critical bibliography, pp. 206–21.)

Gassner, John. *The Theatre in Our Times*. New York: Crown, 1954. Pp. 342–59.

Hurrell, John D., ed. *Two Modern American Tragedies*. New York: Scribner's, 1961.

Jackson, Esther M. *The Broken World of Tennessee Williams*. Madison: University of Wisconsin Press, 1965.

Maxwell, Gilbert. *Tennessee Williams and Friends*. Cleveland: World, 1965.

Nelson, Benjamin. *Tennessee Williams: The Man and His Work*. New York: Ivan Obolensky, 1961.

Tischler, Nancy M. *Tennessee Williams: Rebellious Puritan*. New York: Citadel Press, 1961.

Weales, Gerald. *American Drama since World War II*. New York: Harcourt, Brace, and World, 1962.

Williams, Edwina Dakin (as told to Lucy Freeman). *Remember Me to Tom*. New York: Putnam's, 1963. (Contains many Williams letters.)